"Oh, ring for Liberty!"   "Oh, ring for Liberty!"

S0-CNG-479

The
LIBERTY BELL

The Liberty Bell is one of the most famous symbols of The United States of America. But it had a difficult time surviving from the very beginning.

When the United States was still a colony belonging to Great Britain and Pennsylvania was not a state but a province, transportation and communication were very different. People traveled on land by horse or horse pulled carriages and on water by boat. They sent messages with those people but if they needed to send a very quick message to all the people in the town at one time, they rang a large bell. That is because they had no TVs, no radios, and no telephones. The bell told the people of all the important events.

The ringing of the bell could mean that someone important had died. Then it would be rung muffled (softly). It could be rung quickly or slowly depending on whether or not there was an emergency, like a fire. A certain number of rings might tell the people the time or about a meeting. It might tell them about the arrival of a ship or an important visitor. It might just remind them to come and pray.

The people in the province of Pennsylvania wanted a bell for their State House. This government building had been built in 1732. But before a bell could be hung, a steeple (tower), above the building had to be built. Construction of the steeple began in 1749 and two years later, Isaac Norris, Speaker of the Assembly, ordered a bell with a loud peel (ring) so it could be heard at a great distance.

$\mathcal{A}$lthough there were no bell foundries (factories) in Philadelphia, there were some in New England but Norris ordered the bell from Great Britain, where all the other local bells had been made. The job went to Thomas Lester at the Whitechapel Bell Foundry in London.

LIBERTY BELL.

To make a bell, molds are built. The inner mold is called the core and the outer mold is called the cope. Hot molten (liquid) metal, about 3/4 copper and 1/4 tin is poured between the core and the cope and it hardens as it cools. The inscription (words) are shaped in reverse in the mold. When it is removed from the pit, it is almost black . It is polished and a clapper (ringer) is attached. The bell has a thick lip at the bottom where the clapper strikes. Most of the surface of the bell above the lip is called the waist. The inscription is written on the shoulder, above the waist. And the top is called the crown. The crown is attached by loops or holes, called cannons, to hang the bell from the yoke (frame or holder). A bell sound is made first when the clapper hits the lip of the bell but it continues to reverberate (echo) and creates a rich chord. The inside must be smooth to create the best sound.

Rocky B.

The bell arrived toward the end of the summer in 1752. Before it was hung in the new steeple, it was tested. When the clapper clanged against the bell, the bell broke. This break is NOT the famous crack we recognize in the Liberty Bell. Norris wrote a letter to the Whitechapel foundry complaining that the bell had been too brittle. The foundry responded by saying it was not their fault and that no other bell they had ever made cracked while testing. Some believe that the bell may have cracked during the rough crossing of the Atlantic Ocean to America.

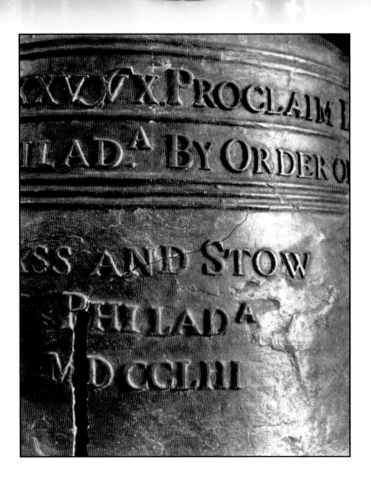

Edmund Woolley had been in charge of the construction at the Pennsylvania State House. He tried but was unable to repair the bell. But he did locate John Stow, a Philadelphia businessman who ran a brass foundry. Brass is a metal made up mostly of copper and zinc. Woolley hired Stow along with John Pass, to recast (remake) the bell.

In order to remelt the bell, it had to be smashed and broken into small pieces. Pass and Stow decided to add some extra copper to the melted bell before it was reshaped. When it was complete in April, it was rung for the members of the Assembly to hear. There were many complaints that the sound was poor, some said because there was too much copper. Pass and Stow were given another chance to remake the bell. In June, the bell later to be known as the Liberty Bell, made by Pass and Stow was finished, approved, and raised to the steeple of the State House. In spite of this, Norris ordered another bell from Whitechapel in Great Britain because he and some others didn't like the sound of the Pass & Stow bell. When the second Whitechapel bell from England arrived, it was placed in the cupola on the roof, and attached to the clocks in order to ring the hours (tell the people the time). The Pass and Stow bell soon became known as the Old One and was used for ringing special occasions.

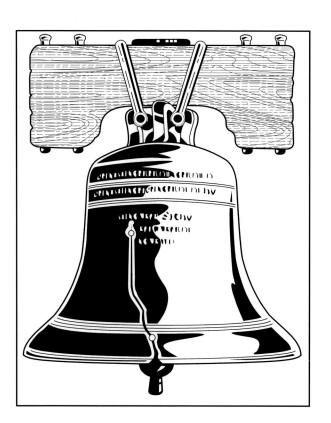

$\mathcal{T}$he Old One had an inscription, "Proclaim liberty throughout all the land unto all the inhabitants thereof." Some people thought that is why the bell became known as the Liberty Bell. The inscription is from the Bible, Leviticus XXV, 10. The bell was ordered to celebrate the 50th anniversary of the Charter of Privileges of 1701. But the inscription on the original bell was 1752, 51 years after the Charter. The Pass and Stow bell says 1753, the year it was recast in Philadelphia. It is one of the mysteries about the bell.

$\mathcal{A}$nother mystery is the 'misspelling' of Pennsylvania on the bell. It is spelled with one "n." At that time (the 18th century), Pennsylvania was not universally adopted. Pennsylvania was named for William Penn. Sylvania means "woods," so Pennsylvania means "Penn's woods." Inscribed on the bell is the quotation, "By Order of the Assembly of the Province of Pennsylvania for the State House in Philda." The choice of the quotation was made by Quaker Isaac Norris, speaker of the assembly.

The Pass and Stow bell or "the Old One" rang to call the Pennsylvania Assembly together on August 27, 1753. It rang when George III became King of England. It tolled (rang) to announce the end of the French and Indian War and to approve the sending of money to support the king. It rang when Benjamin Franklin left for Europe. But in 1764, it began ringing more often to tell of the complaints of the colonists (people who lived in the lands that belonged to England). Most of the complaints had to do with taxes that were added to things that were bought here like tea and sugar. Colonists were angry since they had to pay extra for stuff without having any say about it. This is called, "taxation without representation."

The Liberty Bell did not ring on

July 4, 1776.

Independence was declared on July 4, 1776, but it was a closed meeting and the people did not know what had happened yet. The Declaration of Independence was sent to the printer. Many years later, an author named George Lippard told a story about an old bellman (bell ringer) who was waiting in the tower while his grandson listened at the State House door on July 4th. When the boy heard the news, he rushed to the tower and yelled, "Ring, Grandfather, Ring." It is a good story but is not true. There are many legends and tales about the bell.

When the Declaration of Independence was read on July 8, 1776, at noon by Colonel John Nixon, city bells rang out. The man who probably rang the Old One was Andrew McNair, the paid bell ringer that year for the Pennsylvania State House. It was certainly rung on July 4, 1777, to celebrate the first birthday of the new country, The United States of America.

$\mathcal{B}$ut danger was near. The British Army was heading toward Philadelphia. In September, all the bells of the city were taken down and carted away to be hidden. Some speculate the bells were hidden because of their value, others to prevent communication.

In October 1777, the British occupied Philadelphia. Weeks earlier all the Bells, including the Liberty Bell were removed from the city. It was a large job to lower the heavy bells from their steeples. Instead of carrying it out with soldiers, the Old One was placed on a farmer's cart and covered with hay as it headed north. On the way, the wagon joined with many other wagons for protection. In the small town of Bethlehem, the wagon broke and the bell was moved to another wagon and carted to Allentown (then called Northampton). In Allentown, it was stored in the basement of the Zion Reformed Church, with many other bells.

A year later, the British evacuated (left) Philadelphia and soon after, the Old One and the other bells were brought back. It was returned to the tower where it stayed for three more years. But the wooden tower was rotting and had to be torn down. A temporary roof over the brick part of the tower was built and a new frame was made for the Old One.

In 1799, the capital of Pennsylvania was moved from Philadelphia to Lancaster. A year later, the U.S. capital was also moved from Philadelphia. It was moved to the District of Columbia. The second floor of the "Old" Pennsylvania State House was rented to Charles Wilson Peale who opened a museum of natural history there. Then in 1816, the City bought the State House (bell included) from the state. A new steeple was planned, larger than the original. A new clock would be on it. A new bell, twice as large as the Old One was ordered. The new bell was cast by John Wilbank and hoisted (raised) up to the steeple while the Old One stayed in the brick part of the tower.

LIBERTY BELL

"Oh, ring for Liberty!"   *"Oh, ring for Liberty!"*

*A*nother mystery about the bell was when it cracked. Some say it began to crack when it tolled loud and long for Marquis de Lafayette. As a young French soldier fighting with George Washington, Lafayette quickly rose to major general. He was wounded at Brandywine, wintered at Valley Forge, and assisted in the final surrender at Yorktown. When he returned, almost 50 years after he first arrived, there was a great celebration. The most popular legend was that it cracked in 1835 while tolling for the death of America's great Chief Justice of the Supreme Court, John Marshall. In early 1846, an attempt was made to repair the bell but the crack got longer after it tolled for George Washington's birthday that year. After that, the bell was too cracked to toll and it remained silent.

GRAHAM'S MAGAZINE.

L. XLIV.　　PHILADELPHIA, JUNE, 1854.　　No.

The Bellman informed of the passage of the Declaration of Independence. (See page 562.)

The Liberty Bell probably started to be known by its name in the late 1830's. An anti-slavery pamphlet entitled Liberty, showed a picture of a bell that looked like the Old One on its cover. Soon after, another abolitionist (anti-slavery) pamphlet included a poem, "The Liberty Bell." This poem was reprinted in the magazine, The Liberator. The story about the old bellman and his grandson appeared during this era (time period). As it became more popular, tourists began visiting it more and more.

For over 20 years, the Liberty Bell, as it was now called, was on display in the Assembly Room in the Old Pennsylvania State House. That building was now being called Independence Hall because the Declaration of Independence had been signed there. Then the bell moved around the building. It was hung from a chain with thirteen links in the Tower Room. For a while it was enclosed in a glass case. Then it was removed so people could touch it.

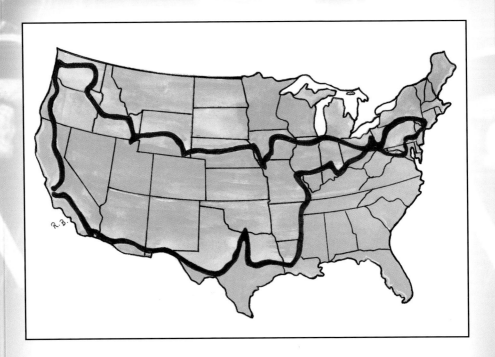

As America grew, people in other parts of the country wanted the chance the see the Liberty Bell in person. Beginning in 1885, for 30 years, the Liberty Bell traveled about 25,000 miles, around the United States. It went to fairs and expositions in New Orleans, Chicago, Atlanta, Charleston, Boston, St. Louis, and San Francisco. As it traveled from Philadelphia to each of these places, it could be seen along the route in the country's cities and towns. It even stopped in Allentown, 116 years after it had been hidden there during the Revolutionary War.

$\mathcal{A}$fter a while, the City of Philadelphia, which owned the bell decided it would be best for it to remain at home. It did travel through the streets of Philadelphia to celebrate Founders' Week in 1908. It made two local trips, one to sell Liberty Loans during World War I, the other to welcome home some of the soldiers after the war.

1915 was the last time the Liberty Bell actually left the city. But its tone was heard on the Pacific Coast when it was tapped and its sound amplified (strengthened) to mark the beginning of cross-country telephone service. It was also tapped with a mallet (a soft hammer, usually rubber or wood) on Ben Franklin's 225th birthday and George Washington's 200th.

World War II had three important taps, one to celebrate D-Day (the landing of American and Allied [America's friends] soldiers in France, another to celebrate the victory in Europe, and a third to celebrate the victory in Japan and the end of the war.

To preserve the Bell, this is not done anymore.

*B*ut it wasn't always famous like the Statue of Liberty, a gift from France. And it wasn't meant to be a memorial like the many monuments and memorials in Philadelphia, Washington, and in towns and cities throughout the United States. The bell we call the Liberty Bell was just a bell, like many others, manufactured to serve a very practical purpose. It rang for special events. It was also used as a means of sending information. It was about one hundred years before the Bell began to become the symbol of freedom that it is today.

The bell was moved the last time to the Liberty Bell Center in November1, 2003.

LIBERTY BELL

"Oh, ring for Liberty!" *"Oh, ring for Liberty!"*

LIBERTY BELL STATISTICS

- circumference around the lip: 2 ft.

- circumference around the crown: 7 ft. 6 in.

- lip to crown: 3 ft.

- height over the crown: 2 ft. 3 in.

- thickness at lip: 3 in.

- weight (originally): 2,080 lbs.

- length of clapper: 3 ft. 2 in.

- weight of clapper: 44.5 lbs.

- weight of yoke: 200 lbs.

- Length of visible hairline fracture: approx. 2 ft. 4 in.

- Length of drilled crack: approx. 2 ft. 5 in.

- yoke wood: American Elm (a.k.a. slippery elm)

Hushed the people's swelling murmur,

Whilst the boy cries joyously;

"Ring!" he's shouting,

"Ring, Grandfather,

Ring! Oh, ring for Liberty!"

Quickly at the given signal

The old bellman lifts his hand.